The Ultimate Beginners Guide on How to Create A Massive Passive Income Monthly with KDP

by Neo Monefa

Table of Contents

9. THANK YOU FOR READING!

1. INTRODUCTION

Technology has brought many innovations and conveniences in the past decade that has enabled individuals to pursue their passions more fervently by making creative avenues more accessible to those who seek them.

There are now wide varieties of gadgets and programs that allow users to have an easy and sometimes direct access to the source of their interests without having to leave their seats. Music fans can now purchase their favorite artists' records through online music stores such as the iTunes Store or Amazon using their iPods, while art aficionados can view and purchase an up-and-coming artist's latest painting from their official websites through netbooks.

Literature enthusiasts are not to be left behind. Online shopping centers like Amazon and eBay are known to sell physical copies of books and magazines which they ship to buyers worldwide and for a long time, this was the most popular way for readers to gain access to copies of literature that may not be available in their local bookstores.

While effective, this method posed a lot of problems in terms of shipping times and costs, which developed a craving for a more practical and wireless approach to literature publishing and distribution.

What is Kindle?

Today's modern technologies make it easier for authors, publishers and even aspiring writers to make their materials more accessible to their audiences than ever before. Some say that it will bring the death of physical books that can be bought in brick-and-mortar bookstores and shops while others insist that the Kindle will revive interest in literature.

Whatever the case may be, it is evident that the Kindle has been widely accepted all over the world as a convenient way to access books, articles, newspapers and other written material in digital form in one lightweight and compact p device.

Essentially, the Kindle is an electronic book reader conceptualized by Amazon.com, a website that specializes in selling goods online. It allows its users to browse and download a wide variety of digital content ranging from novels to magazines using an Internet connection.

There is an estimated 900,000 titles currently available in the Kindle Store that Kindle users can download and read, depending on a title's distribution agreement. Readers can access their purchased content in a matter of minutes, eliminating the waiting period to receive physical copies in the mail. Because digital copies are produced without paper and printing, the prices are also generally lower than in bookstores, both offline and online.

The average price for an e-book can range between $0.99 to $14.99 depending on the title and author, with new bestsellers from major publishing companies like MacMillan costing somewhere between $12.99 to $15. Alternatively, lesser known authors and first-time writers can offer their content for less than a dollar while some publish free titles.

With 700,000 titles to choose from, there is no shortage of content from a wide variety of topics in the Kindle Store with an equally wide variety of prices and terms for each download.

We will be exploring e-book purchases in greater detail in later chapters. For now, let's look into the history of the Kindle so far.

The History of Kindle

To satiate and address the need for a more effective and cost-efficient method of delivering copies of books, newspapers and magazines to readers all over the world, Amazon.com has conceptualized the Kindle, which was developed by its subsidiary Lab 126.

The original Amazon Kindle was released in 2007, which was welcomed by the public with equal parts of curiosity and pessimism. It should be noted that in terms of gadgets and consumer technology, the years of 2006-2007 was dominated by Apple products such as the iPhone and the iPod Touch, making the entry of the Kindle even more interesting.

Kindle Versions and Releases

Kindle I

Despite the uphill battle for a slice of the tech market, the first version of Kindle did exceptionally well and was received with much fanfare. Within five and a half hours, the Kindle – exclusively released on Amazon.com, of course – was sold out and it took almost five months before it was restocked.

Kindle 2

In 2009, Amazon announced that it will release the Kindle 2, a new and improved version of the original that was released two years prior. Additional features, as well as functional improvements were added to the newest version. The best-selling author Stephen King even helped in promoting the product by releasing his latest novel entitled UR exclusively on Kindle 2. Despite the rolling success of this version however, it was discontinued only nine months after it was released, replacing it with the international version of the Kindle 2.

Although physically similar to the US-only version, the main difference of the international version of the Kindle 2 from the original is its mobile network standard, which allows users from 100 different countries to download content and titles. Many reviews from notable gadget websites such as Gadget Lab often criticized the second generation Kindle for having a higher contrast screen that made it difficult to read small-sized fonts, which are regularly used in e-books. Despite these criticisms, the Kindle 2 (the US and international versions combined) went on to sell more units than the original Kindle.

The Kindle DX

The next Kindle version to be released was named the Kindle DX, which was made available to the public in 2009. To date, the Kindle DX is the thinnest version to be released, with the physical measurements of 10.4" x 7.2" x 0.38" or about the same size of most magazines.

Many critics and even loyalists complain about the overly large screen, which makes it seem like a tablet but without the apps and functionalities to go with it. Many fans however love the bigger screen size, which makes it easier for them to breeze through their downloaded content.

A year later, Amazon released the Kindle DX Graphite, which saw the signature white casing of the four versions turn to a grayish black. The E Ink displays the main feature of this version, which improves the contrast ratio by 50%. The dark-colored encasing is also believed to improve the screen contrast, making it easier for users to read content.

Size Matters: A side-by-side comparison of the Kindle 2 and the Kindle DX shows the size difference between the two versions.

Kindle Keyboard

Wasting no time in getting the latest in e-book reader technology to the consumers, Amazon released the Kindle Keyboard on August 2010. This version branches out to two more versions: the Kindle Wi-Fi and the Kindle 3G + Wi-Fi.

Both Kindle Keyboard versions came in two different colors: white and graphite. It is also smaller than its predecessor, the Kindle DX. The new and smaller design has made holding the device for long periods more comfortable than the previous versions, and the six-inch screen was also enhanced to improve readability and screen contrast.

The first ad-supported Kindle also began with these versions, which lowered the standard retail price from $139 to $114 for the Wi-Fi only units. Other special offers were also included later on which further reduced the unit price to only $99.

Kindle 4 aka Kindle Touchless

The first to debut in the Fourth Generation line of Kindle devices is the Kindle 4, which is the most affordable version to date. With the introductory rate of $79 when it came out, many Kindle Keyboard users considered ditching their older devices in lieu of the lighter and smaller Kindle 4.

Unlike all of the earlier versions, the Kindle 4 has no keyboard or a touch screen functionality, which made it very difficult for users to search for e-books in the Kindle Library or to use the device as a web browser. Navigating and typing is solely dependent on the five-way controller, which requires a lot of patience and familiarity for the user to be able to maximize the Kindle 4.

Kindle Touch

The Kindle Touch is the first touch screen device of the Kindle brand that had a lot of observers wondering what the delay was in entering the touch screen world that was already being used extensively by other competitors' devices.

It is widely accepted though that the quality of the Kindle Touch's touch screen is well worth the wait. The Kindle Touch comes with 4GB of internal storage space with a battery life that could last up to two months on a single full charge. Users can also choose between a Wi-Fi only device and a unit that can connect to the Internet through either Wi-Fi or 3G networks.

Kindle Fire

The Kindle Fire is the last of the Fourth Generation line that was also released in September 2011 along with the Kindle 4 and the Kindle Touch. Another first for Kindle, this version has a color touch screen and runs using the Android OS.

Now more than just a humble e-book reader, the Kindle Fire functions' expand to web browsing, movie and video watching, music listening and game playing. In short, the Kindle Fire is now more like a tablet device than an e-book reader and not a lot of people are complaining about the added features.

The Kindle Fire retails at $199 with Wi-Fi connectivity only, a lot cheaper than Apple's iPad, which sells for $499. With Amazon Prime membership, a user can have access to 50,000 bestselling e-books that they can "borrow" free of charge. Unlike libraries though, there are no due dates.

2. THE BASICS: KINDLE AND E-BOOKS

Despite's Kindle's departure from being a dedicated e-book reader in its last version – the Kindle Fire, it's main purpose and function is still centered around electronic books, digital versions of publications and newsprints and from the Kindle DX version onwards, academic and personal publications that are in PDF format.

However, if you want to make money off of Kindle content, it's practical to know the potentials and limitations of the devices so that you can maximize your offering. The extra features may allow you to package what you're selling more effectively which would greatly help in increasing your profits.

The next sub-chapter will explore the different key features of the Amazon Kindles.

Noteworthy Features of the Kindle

Being able to sell millions of device is not an easy feat but is something that Amazon has been doing with ease ever since the first version of Kindle came out. Of course not all the admiration is without merit. Consumers purchase the Kindle because it satisfies their e-book reader needs better than other e-book readers in the market.

Let's look at the different features of the Amazon Kindle that millions of users all over the world love and appreciate.

Access to thousands of e-books through the Kindle Store.

Bestsellers and obscure titles alike can be browsed and downloaded from the Kindle Store. Users will be able to see the cover art and e-book description before making a purchase, much like anyone would in a real bookstore.

Moreover, there are other applications or "apps" that allows Kindle users to download a title from their own selection of content. With this much title choices, it's nearly impossible to not find a book, magazine or article worth downloading.

Versions: All Kindle versions

Portability

Imagine being able to carry hundreds, even thousands of books with you wherever you go. Kindle has made it easier for book lovers to bring with them all of their favorite titles and must-read literature no matter where they go without having to allot massive amounts of space in their bags or luggage. Kindle users no longer have to decide which books in their collection to take on an intimate vacation or on their daily commute to work. Every piece of downloaded reading material is secured in one place.

Version: All Kindle versions

Easy-to-use e-book search and browsing functions.

The available e-books are categorized according to their genres, authors or titles making it extremely easy even for non-"techy" users to navigate through the Kindle Library. Unlike in bookstores where shoppers will have to walk around the store in order to find the title they're looking for, Kindle only needs its users to either use the control pad or touch screen to browse through the titles lists.

Versions: All kindle versions

Text-to-Speech function

For users wanting to give their tired eyes some rest or for individuals who have reading disabilities, Kindle has an optional feature that would allow you to relax and have the device do the heavy-lifting. Kindle has a "read to me" function that will enable the device to "read aloud" the text of the book or periodical that you wish to read.

This feature is not available on all titles however as certain publishers may opt out of this function.

Versions: Kindle 2, Kindle 3, Kindle DX (both versions), Kindle Touch

Web Browsing

For users on the go, being able to browse the Internet (and not just device-specific locations) is a necessary feature. Kindle allows its users to choose between two kinds of connections: Wi-Fi or 3G. With later versions, Kindle users will be able to check their e-mail, make web searches or access non-Amazon websites on their devices.

Versions: Wi-Fi – Kindle 3, Kindle Touch, Kindle Fire   3G – Kindle 2, Kindle 3

Note Taking and Cloud Storage

For ardent book lovers, it is not unusual to want to scribble down notes on book margins to capture thoughts and ideas. With Kindle, you'll be able to add text annotations, highlight important phrases or quotations and bookmark poignant pages for future reference. All the notes can be saved, edited, deleted or shared to your family and friends who also uses Kindle.

Kindle Notes: A convenient way to digitally save your thoughts and musings.

You may also save all your Amazon-related content on your Cloud Storage to save or expand your existing device storage. You'll be able to access your Cloud Storage using your Amazon account.

Versions: Kindle DX, Kindle 3, Kindle 4, Kindle Touch, Kindle Fire

Whispersync

Kindle's Whispersync allows you to access your Kindle books from multiple devices such as your iPhone or iPod Touch, Android devices, Blackberry phones or tablet and your PC or Mac. The Whispersync function saves your reading progress across all devices enabling you to continue reading in another device where you left off on a different device.

Versions: Kindle 2, Kindle 3, Kindle DX, Kindle 4, Kindle Touch, Kindle Fire

Document Reader

Professional and important documents can also be stored and accessed on the Amazon Kindle which you can also share via e-mail to your approved contacts, eliminating the need for printing. PDF and Word documents can be shared and accessed through your personal Kindle library on Amazon using any web browser. You can also convert documents into the standard Kindle format to make them appear like your Kindle books.

Versions: Kindle 2 (PDF conversion only) Kindle DX, Kindle 3, Kindle 4, Kindle Touch, Kindle Fire

These are just a few of Amazon Kindle's features that make them distinct and well-loved among its users. Each Kindle version contains different features that may not be available in others so if you're looking for a specific function, be careful to review the features before purchasing a Kindle device.

Now that you are more familiar with what Kindle has to offer, let's look at the different e-books and content that can be browsed, downloaded and accessed on a Kindle so that you'll have an idea of how your e-book should be constructed.

Types of E-Books and Downloadable Content Supported by Kindle

Not all e-books are created equal and Kindle does not support all known and available e-book formats. If your plan on writing and publishing your own e-book that Kindle users will be able to access, download and read, you'll need to know which formats are suitable for your e-book before you release it.

Luckily, Kindle supports a wide range of e-book formats and for the formats that are not compatible, Kindle has file conversion tools that would make the book readable on the device and the Kindle App.

When it comes to e-books, these are the e-book formats that can be read natively (as is) on the Kindle:

• AZW. E-books purchased and downloaded from the Kindle Library or Kindle Store will come in this format, as well as other material purchased from Amazon. If you want to ensure maximum readability for your readers, opt to publish your e-book in this format. In later chapter, you will learn how to convert your document file into the AZW format.

• MOBI/PRC. The MOBI format was developed by the French company Mobipocket which is now owned by Amazon. The AZW is actually based from this format with the main difference being the serial number scheme. MOBI documents and e-books can be read as is on the Kindle so you could consider this format as an alternative of the AZW for your e-book.

The MOBI format follows an open eBook standard that uses XHTML language and may include JavaScript and frames. Only MOBI and PRC e-books that do not have Digital Rights Managament (DRM) protection can be read on the Kindle.

Portable Document Format (PDF). A large number of documents and e-books are published in this format though readability on the Kindle is still being improved. Aside from Kindle, plenty of e-book readers also support this format. If you intend to publish scientific or academic journals and articles on Kindle, this is an ideal format to adopt.

Plain Text (TXT). This is the simplest and least decorated or formatted format that can be used on the Kindle. Although completely readable on the device, most authors prefer to use other formats as TXT files lack formatting and do not appear professional.

Other documents, e-books and materials that are in other formats can be easily converted to any of the four main formats that Kindle is compatible with. There are plenty of apps and websites that offer file conversion tools for free.

Browsing the Kindle Store

In order to enjoy the Kindle reading experience, you'll need to download or purchase an e-book. You can browse through different available titles using the Kindle device or by going to Amazon.com on your computer to access the Kindle Store.

Via Device

Connecting to and browsing the Amazon Store is easy using the Kindle device. One advantage of using the device to purchase content is that it downloads and stores the content directly on the device wirelessly.

To browse the Kindle Store:
• Connect to the Internet.
• Press/touch/scroll to the 'Menu' button to make the menu list appear.
• Choose the 'Shop in Kindle Store' option.

You will be taken to the Browse page where you can choose between types of publications. Simply select the type of content that you wish to download or use the Search function to find content quickly.

Once you've chosen your e-book, click on 'Buy' to complete the purchase.
The e-book will be delivered to your device wirelessly through Amazon Whispernet.

If you purchase an e-book by mistake, you have the option to cancel and refund the purchase immediately after the content is bought.

Via Amazon.com

Alternatively, you can also purchase Kindle e-books through Amazon's shopping site.
Type www.amazon.com on your web browser.
On the home page, you can immediately use the search function at the top of the page to make finding your content more convenient. Choose the 'Kindle Store' as your search department.

On the other hand, you can bring out the drop down menu on the left side of the page by hovering on the 'Kindle' tab and selecting 'Kindle Books.'

You'll be taken to the Kindle E-Book Store landing page where you'll see the day's bestsellers. Again you can use the search function at the top of the page to find what you're looking for quicker or you can use the tags and links at the left-side of the page to browse titles in different genres.
Once you find the title that you're looking for, click on the 'Buy now with 1-Click' icon on the right-side of the page and choose where the e-book will be delivered. You can have it delivered to your Kindle Cloud Reader or your registered Kindle device.

3. KINDLE AND MONEY-MAKING

From November to the end to 2011, Amazon was selling up to one million Kindle devices per week, creating an e-book market never seen before. Amazon is not the only winner with the Kindle's success. Both major and indie publishers have also seen a massive growth in the sales of their e-books and other digital materials.

Aspiring authors and content writers can now publish their literary works without the backing of a major publication house. Distribution is no longer a major roadblock to literary success as the Kindle Store can be accessed wirelessly from anywhere in the world.

Introduction to E-Book Writing

With the development and popularity of e-book readers, many famous authors have given in to the clamor of owning digital copies of their famous books and novels and have seen their sales skyrocket. Publishers earned $69.9 million in e-book sales from January to February of 2011 alone.

Amazon has reported that e-books have outsold printed books in 2011 for the first time in history. According to the sales analysis released by Amazon, for every 100 printed book bought in 2011, 105 e-books were sold. From January to October of the previous year, e-book sales rose by 131% with $807 million worth of e-books sold. Of the total e-book sales in 2011, up to 38% was purchased from Amazon.

Those staggering figures also reflect the major publishers' publishing preferences. More and more publishing houses realize the potential for sales and profits in ebooks, not to mention the low production costs involved compared to publishing printed material.

So how does this publishing trend relate to you as a writer? Essentially, Kindle allows the publishing of digital written material through Kindle Direct Publishing which we will discuss in greater detail in later chapters. Once an e-book or title is published, it can be browsed and bought by Kindle users all over the world. Indie publishing is another popular trend in the e-book world and with good material and promotion, you could earn hundreds, even thousands of dollars through the sales of your e-book.

Now back to e-book writing

If high-quality e-book writing is not as easy as it sounds. With easy publishing on Kindle, the market for good e-books are now heavily congested with stiff competition and if you want to differentiate yourself as a writer from the rest, you'll have to bring something extra special to the table.

In later chapters we'll be looking at different ways to make your e-book unique and interesting. Remember, the best way to sell a book is by offering something that your audience can't live without and we will be exploring the different techniques to do exactly that later on.

Introduction to E-Book Publishing for Kindle

Publishing your own written work has never been easier with Kindle and in the ebook world, this ease has its own pros and cons.

The Good News

Publishing digital content on Kindle allows writers from all over the world to make their works available for public consumption easily, wirelessly and quickly – without having to rely on major publishers or distribution partners.

You are making your material available to millions of Kindle users all over the world. If making money is your main agenda, imagine having that big of a market in your fingertips.

You have complete creative control when you self-publish. If you choose to outsource your pre-publishing preparations, you may get recommendations on the direction, flow or style of your material but the publication of your content is not dependent on whether you apply those recommendations or not.

You will earn 35%-70% of your retail price for every copy of your material that you sell on the Amazon Store. It may seem like a small amount but bear in mind that major publishers usually offer only 5%-15% of the listed price in royalties.

Speaking of retail prices, with Amazon publishing, you can set the monetary value of your work yourself. You can price your e-book the amount that you think it deserves.
Kindle publishing is not without criticism though and before you take the plunge to the world of self or indie publishing, it's best to know about what's on the other side of the coin.

The Not-So-Good News

As previously mentioned, the competition is stiff in the Kindle e-book industry. Kindle users can choose from thousands of titles and if your material is mediocre, unpolished or common, your material will simply be overlooked and passed over.

Piracy is always a big issue with digital content and e-books are no exceptions. Sly pirates have a variety of means and methods in order to share content to their friends and families without having to pay for copies. With Kindle however, it's not such a big problem as they use a propriety format that disallows a user from reading your e-book on another device owned by someone else.

The promotion of your e-book is largely your responsibility. Although Kindle has made numerous marketing and promotion promises to authors over the years, it has not really translated for many amateur authors and first-time publishers.

Succeeding in e-book sales poses a real challenge to inexperienced writers who have never had any material published in the past, but at the same time it has also introduced obscure yet talented authors to literature enthusiasts.

In order to defy the many speed bumps in the e-book industry, you'll need to know how to create sellable materials. If you're up for the challenge, move on to the next chapter to see how you can write profitable e-books.

4. WRITING CONTENT THAT SELLS

Producing unique content could mean the difference between making money and going unnoticed in the e-book industry. With thousands of titles already being sold in the Kindle Store, you will have to come up with something that readers have never seen before in order to successfully breach the congested e-book market.

This chapter will guide you on how to create a memorable e-book that will have readers gushing and wanting more.

E-Books and Kindle Singles

Before diving into the writing process, it's best to first determine whether you'll be able to produce a complete and lengthy e-book, or if a shorter and more concise publication will be more ideal for the amount of material that you have.
In Kindle publication, you have the option of writing complete literary works or instructional e-books or you can publish shorter publications which are referred to as a Kindle Single. Let's look into both formats.

E-Books. Essentially, an e-book is a full-length publication that is simply the digital version of a book that can be published in different file formats and read in compatible readers or devices. As in a printed publication, it may contain text or images or a combination of both.

The main characteristic of e-books is its length and while Amazon does not have a set word count requirement, many readers generally steers clear of short publications that are marketed as e-books.

Best adopted for: novels, biographies and autobiographies, academic text books, memoirs, coffee table books, children's books, literary collections, dictionaries, travel guides, manuals, general reference materials, screenplays

Kindle Single. Amazon launched the Kindle Single format on October 2010 with much excitement. Compared to e-books, Kindle Single publications are shorter, with a word count range of 5,000 to 30,000 which is roughly equivalent to 30-90 pages.

Kindle Singles also has different royalty options from traditional e-books which we will be exploring in later chapters.

Best adopted for: short stories, concise cook books, poetry books, academic reports, essays, short memoirs, quotation collections, short fictions, short literary series, and opinion pieces.

Choosing Your Topic

After deciding which type of content you want to publish, the next major task is to choose a subject or topic for your e-book or Single. Consider this as the foundation of the entire e-book writing process from which everything else stems. The importance of this step cannot be said enough. Your writing style may be a selling point in itself but without substance, you'll be hard-pressed to sell enough copies to make a profit.

It's not enough to just settle with a topic, you will want to choose topics that people want to know more about. If a person is interested in a subject like parenting for example, expect that person to actively look for reading materials that are directly related to the subject. If you are looking at e-book writing as a source of income, producing material that you KNOW people are looking for would ensure that your ebook (or article) will be bought again and again.

E-books specifically published for profit follows slightly different techniques in topic selection.
Keyword Searches. The World Wide Web has become a repository of information about any topic imaginable and narrowing down the list to the subjects that are most frequently searched for will give your material a higher chance of getting purchased.

Most search engines have a keyword suggestion tool that will give you information about the most searched for topics and keywords. Writing about a popular topic will increase the likelihood of your e-book (or Single) to be searched for in the Amazon Store.

Use Amazon.com as a Research Tool. Browsing Amazon.com will give you an idea of what types or genres of e-books people are buying. Knowing the trends in e-books will give you an advantage of being able to publish what the Kindle users are downloading. Amazon.com is also a valuable tool to help you in the pricing of your materials.

Bestsellers: You can check out the bestselling e-books on the Kindle Store in
Amazon's website. You can also search for the bestselling books in a specific genre by clicking on the links at the left side of the page.

Lurk in Forums and Bulletin Boards. Reading through message boards is like being a fly on the wall. You will be able to know more about the issues, subjects and discussions that people feel passionately about, which would help you determine a topic that is interesting to other people.

Most message boards and forums offer free membership while others maintain open threads that would allow you to read discussions without having to sign up.

Personal Experiences and Interests. Nothing can inspire great writing better than the subjects and topics that you have passion for. Explore your own thoughts and proclivities and you'll be able to find a specific topic that you would enjoy writing about and sharing to readers who may share the same interests or would want to know more about it.

Spend some time brain-storming and listing down your interests then narrow down the topics to your absolute favorites. Choose two or three subjects that you feel strongly about then ask for feedback from family or friends.

There are literally (no pun intended) millions of possible topics and subjects to choose from so don't limit yourself. Get other people involved in your creative process and don't be afraid to ask for their opinions and thoughts. You'll never know when and where a light-bulb moment will strike so be open to all possibilities.

The Do's and Don'ts of Kindle E-Book Writing

E-book writing is not an easy task. Not everyone can write, publish and successfully sell an e-book on the Kindle Store but with patience, research and the right preparation, you'll be able to produce a masterpiece that people will want to pay for to read.

E-book writing for Kindle poses a lot of writing challenges because a.) To sell ebooks, you'll need to catch people's attentions and b.) There are already hundreds of writers who are currently selling their own materials on Amazon.

Now is not the time to be disheartened, after all, you've already gotten through the hard task of choosing a topic to write about. Now that you're ready to begin penning down your first e-book, review first what you should and shouldn't do to increase your chances of Kindle e-book success.

Do These

Create an outline for your e-book or Single. Contrary to popular belief, outlines do NOT stifle creativity. In fact, it creates an effective thought process and order to your creative ideas. Outlines are also useful in reminding you of thoughts or topics that you may forget while in the process of writing, making sure that everything that you want to write about will be in your final product.

Write using a word processing program that you're most comfortable with. If you are worried about the compatibility your e-book's format, rest assured that there are plenty of conversion tools that you can use to convert your final product to a Kindle compatible format. If you want to stay on the safe side, use MS Word.

Try to steer clear of typewriters

Proofread! There is nothing more annoying to excited readers than unedited books. Misspelled words, wrong grammar and irritating formatting will turn a reader OFF and it will be a nearly impossible task to turn them back on. If you spend a lot of time surfing the Internet and reading web content that allows commenting, you'll see how some people take it upon themselves to correct posts with grammatical and spelling errors.

The "Grammar Police" as they are often called are also present in the Kindle Universe. Though they cannot publicly comment and point out your language mistakes instantly, they can however give you a bad review which is bad for business.

The importance of proofreading cannot be stressed enough which is why there is an entire chapter dedicated this life-saving process. We'll get into that later.

Adopt your own e-book style. Whether it's using your own scribble art for the covers or making up your own language, having a unique style will differentiate you from the other e-book writers. J.R.R Tolkien invented the Elvish language (among other languages) for his Middle-Earth collection of novels. Anthony Burgess created his own words for A Clockwork Orange.

Jostein Gaarder used the deck of playing cards as his chapter headings for The Solitaire Mystery while Theodor "Dr. Seuss" Geisel illustrated most of the artwork used in his published books. Having your own e-book style will generate more interest for your work which this time, is good for business.

Do NOT Do These

Plagiarize. Plagiarism in the publishing world is a death sentence. If your materials is found to be a rip-off of a published work, your e-book will be taken off the Amazon Store and you may be slapped with additional restrictions. You can use Copyscape – an online plagiarism checker – to see whether your work has any duplicates floating around in cyberspace.

Raise your word count with excessive fillers. Readers will know if they're being taken on a literary ride, and not in a good way. Do not feel pressured by word count requirements. Unless you're aiming for a Single publication, let the word count be a secondary consideration and focus more on the substance and readability of your content.

Use copyrighted artworks without acknowledging the artist. If you intend on adding front and back covers with images, or if you want to include pictures on your ebooks, always remember to ask permission from the owners of the images and acknowledge your sources in your e-book. If you own or have the rights to the images, it's still a good practice to share to your readers where the pictures were taken from.

Pressure yourself. If you are an amateur writer, do not burden yourself with unreasonable expectations. Set practical schedules and milestones to guide you into completing your work within a certain duration.

Get discouraged. So your first published work didn't sell millions of copies, what now? Keep writing of course. The thing about writing is that - as in other artistic endeavors, it can be discouraging to hear negative criticisms or receive bad reviews. Don't let this stop you from producing and writing more materials. Practice makes perfect and with every e-book you publish, more experience is gained.

E-book writing is a lengthy process that is both rewarding and frustrating at times. The key to success is to focus on your goal of publishing, selling and profiting from your hard work.

Let us know look at more tips on how to effectively write an e-book that sells.

5 Essential Tips for Effective E-Book Creation

E-books need time to be conceptualized and created in order to ensure maximum customer satisfaction. Writing may simply be an artistic and creative pursuit for some but that doesn't mean that you can't have your readers in mind while putting ideas into work.

If you want to publish an e-book that your readers will enjoy and will make money for you, follow these simple tips to get you started on a successful writing process.

Understand Your Audience's Language

Let's say that you're writing a "for dummies" type of book that explains the concepts of football to clueless newlywed housewives. Being a football enthusiast yourself, you may be tempted to use common football jargon to explain what an Inside Run is.

Using the words "dive," "toss," "tackles" and "line of scrimmage" will not only confuse your targeted readers, it may also alienate them. When using jargon, be sure to explain what those words mean first to guarantee that they can follow your ideas. You can also include a short glossary of terms in your e-book.

The most effective way to get your idea across effectively is to use a writing style or language that your audience is familiar with. Match your e-book to your audience to keep them interested and hooked to your words.

Do Your Research

In previous chapters you learned how to use Internet tools to research your possible e-book topics. When writing, you should use the same research skills you developed to know more about what you are writing about. Feel free to use other tools aside from the Internet. Go to your local library or bookstore to see what other publications are saying about what you're writing about.

You may even request for interviews with established experts in a specific field or ask your family and friends for advice or feedback on a relevant issue. Be creative in your research and you'll be sure to find some knowledge and inspiration.

In order to cement your credibility as a writer, be sure that what you publish only contains factual details if you're writing a manual or guide. For fiction pieces, the real world can provide you with natural human reactions and interactions that would lend authenticity to your novel.

Start With a Draft

Don't pressure yourself to produce a perfect e-book on your first try. It is a common mistake for first-time writers to get hung up on the grammar, spelling, formatting and the other technical side of writing immediately on the initial draft. While this may save you time in proofreading your work later on, it can also disturb your writing momentum or cause you to lose creative ideas before you get the chance to write them down.

Most experienced authors swear by the effectiveness of writing a first draft in ensuring the quality of the final product. On your first draft, just write. You can also choose to ignore your outline for this early version so that you can just concentrate on writing what's on your mind. Many great ideas come from unconstrained mental environments so let your imagination run wild.

Don't worry about your grammar, sentence construction, spelling and verb agreements for this step, just write.

Use Your Outline to Organize Your First Draft

You now have your outline and your first draft, it's time for you to begin piecing your e-book together. For some writers, the process is as simple as using the outline as the guide in forming a cohesive piece using what they wrote in the first draft. For others, this process involves reconstructing the outline to fit the available written materials.

Try to find your own technique in piecing together what you have. Imagine your outline as the table of contents for your book. Don't hesitate to remove or add to your outline as you see fit. There is no set formula to writing and the effectiveness of techniques varies from writer to writer. Explore your own writing process that will enable you to produce a high-quality product.

Read, Read, Read

Good writers include reading in their daily activities. Whether it's reading a newspaper, a sci-fi novel or graphic novels, reading enhances writing. While you're in the process of writing your own e-book, reading other materials can help in improving your vocabulary, expose you to different writing styles and give you tips on how you can improve your own ideas.

You can even re-read your favorite books or simply read web content. The choice is yours to make. Don't look at other publications as competition, take them as constructive research materials. You may also find yourself critiquing other works which is good. In realizing what other books or articles are missing, you'll be able to spot areas that can be improved in your own work in progress.

5. PREPPING YOUR E-BOOK FOR PUBLICATION

Finishing writing your e-book is an exciting achievement. There are many aspiring writers who never get beyond their first drafts and here you are, actually done with the writing process.

So what's next?

Before you publish and sell your e-book on the Amazon Store, you still need to prepare your product for mass selling. With physical books, the writers would submit their final work to the publishers who will then proofread, edit and make recommendations about the saleability of the material. Once everything on the content-side is approved by both the publishers and the writer, front and back covers are chosen and applied, then the entire book with all its parts will be printed and distributed to book stores.

With e-book publishing, the same process is applied but with alterations. First comes the proofreading, then the covers selection, conversion to applicable file formats then the submission to the e-book store or the Amazon Store in this case.

This chapter will explore the different pre-publishing preparation steps to make sure that your e-book will appear professionally made and worth the time (and money) of your target audience.

DIY versus Outsource

Pre-publication preparation is never an easy process, especially if it's your first stab at self-publishing and e-book writing. You may find yourself lost in the entire process at times, not knowing what to do and what to do next. Before you become intimidated with the whole idea of "pre-pub prep," know that you have the option to either do it yourself or to acquire the help and services of specialized companies and organizations that are in the business of proofreading and editing e-books.

If you think that you have the knowledge, skills and means to edit your own work, create your own cover design, layout the e-book and market the complete package then by all means, do it yourself and save time and money. It will also provide you with valuable experience that you'll be able to apply on your next e-book.

On the other hand, if you want professional and highly-experienced e-book specialists to handle the preparation aspects of your e-book, the chances of publishing a well-designed, expertly edited product will increase significantly.

Let's review the different tasks that need to be accomplished before you can publish your e-book and let's see how DIY and outsourcing services will compare.

Do-It-Yourself	Outsource

Editing and Proofreading. This may be difficult to accomplish if you don't have any experience or knowledge in editing. You may also exhibit some bias in your own work which could hinder you from judging the styling and use of words appropriately. You can ask friends, colleagues or relatives who have editing experience to look at your work for you. They will be able to apply appropriate corrections and improvements.

Alternatively, you can hire editors or "book doctors" to do the job for you. There are plenty of qualified professionals who edit books for a living. Also look into hiring freelancers who may ask for lower fees.

Book Cover Designing   If you have knowledge and experience in graphic arts, you will have an advantage in this area. You can also purchase stock photography on the internet or take your own photos.

Even e-books can be judged by its cover art so you'll need to conceptualize and produce a unique and eye catching cover design to make your e-book stand out. You can hire freelancers to do the cover art for you or you can acquire the services of e-book publishing companies that offer complete pre-pub solutions that include book cover designing.

Be prepared to shell out some money though as artists may charge huge amounts depending on the complexity of the concept and art work.

You'll also need to research the different book layouts so that you can get an idea of what an effective layout looks like. This is especially important for manuals and how-to e-books. Actually make this process go faster. Professionals already have their chosen software mastered plus they have the experience to know which layout will fit your content the best.

E-Book File Conversion   File conversions for e-books may seem simple enough but there's still a degree of difficulty to it. You'll need to make sure that when you convert your original e-book to a Kindle-compatible file format, the layout will remain the same. Outsourced professionals may already have tools, programs or software that will make conversion as simple as clicking an icon.

You may also choose to use e-book publishing software that includes copyright protection for your e-book, a text editing program and embedding of flash, Shockwave and other video formats on your e-book.

Front and Back Content

Although not a requirement, Amazon recommends that you add Front and Back written content to give your e-book a more professional look and feel. It's a pretty simple and straightforward inclusion that you'll be able to finish in less than an hour.

For your front pages or front matter, as Amazon calls it, include the following details:

Title Page. This page should contain your e-book title followed by your name on the next line. Have it centered on the page.

Your E-Book Title
Your Name
Copyright Page. This page usually follows the Title Page and contains the copyright details of the e-book.
Title of the E-Book
Copyright: Name of Copyright Owner / © Name of Copyright Owner
Date of E-Book Publication
ISBN (note: if applicable to you. This is not a requirement)
Publisher (note: You can use your name for this field or leave it out completely)

Dedication. If you are dedicating the e-book to someone, include it on the page after the Copyrights. It could be a short message or a simple shout out to your friends and family to a full-length love letter, as long as it fits a single page.

Preface. If you wish to provide an introduction to your e-book or make a statement about the objective and/or creation of the content, use the Preface page. Follow the formatting that you used for the body of your e-book.

Prologue. If you need to establish the setting or location for your e-book or to give little background details to help the readers understand the story better, the Prologue page is where you should put it.

Amazon also recommends adding an ACTIVE table of contents if applicable to the content of your e-book. This should be included after the front matter and before the first chapter. An active table of contents is dynamic and changes its page numbers depending on the size and settings of an individual reader. You can use MS Word's built-in table of contents creator or conversion programs' tools.

For the back matter, there is no set order to how the content should appear and is only included if applicable to the e-book. Back matter can include:

References
Bibliographies
Notes
Glossaries
Appendices

You can choose to omit this part completely if it's not applicable to your content.

Editing and Proofreading

One surefire way to turn your readers off is by subjecting them to a poorly edited ebook. Not only is wrong grammar, incorrect spelling, improper use of words and disjointed ideas in poor taste, it also reflects poorly of you as an author. There are software and programs available over the Internet that you can use to proofread your work but to ensure high-quality products, editing and proofreading is best left to humans.

To give you an idea of how important book editing is, with physical books, it takes up to four reads before a publisher gives the okay for printing. Again, when you're self publishing your e-book, you can edit your work yourself or you can outsource the job to professionals.

If you choose to DIY, here are some helpful self-editing tips:

When you're done with your first draft, take a few days off before you begin editing. This will refresh your mind and help you look at your work with different eyes (so to speak).

When self-editing, do not show anyone your first draft. Resist the urge to get feedback on the first thing you've written. Remember that the first draft is your unpolished and raw work. Negative criticism may end up discouraging you so keep your first draft for your eyes only.

Replace little words such as "was," "it," etc. use your creativity to substitute more constructive words to mundane little ones.

For example, instead of: "Easter Sunday was a tragic day that was the beginning of something dark. It began a spiral into an abyss that was created by the death of something beautiful. It was scary, it still is. It is an unforgettable moment in our family's history that we all want to forget."

You can edit it to: "Easter Sunday was a tragic day that signaled the beginning of something dark. The Gloomy Sunday began a painful spiraling into an abyss created by the death of something beautiful. The memory of Black Easter is etched in the family's collective which we will spend a lifetime trying to erase from our psyches. That day instilled fear in us, a fear that we cannot ignore."

Notice how replacing mediocre words enhanced the mood and improved the imagery of the idea.

Use the CTRL+F function in MS Word to help you find specific words or to see how many times you've used a word. The word "that" is commonly used too often in both prose and instructional works and is something that you'll want to look out for. Eliminating "that" needs no word replacements in most cases and enhances the flow of ideas and sentence structures.

For example: "When I heard that familiar voice on the other end of the line, I knew that I was in trouble. It was at that moment that I realized how low I've sunk and that it will take more than Daddy's hug to get me out of this mess."

Instead: "When I heard that familiar voice on the other end of the line, I knew that I was in trouble. It was at that moment that I realized how low I've sunk and that (how) it will take more than Daddy's hug to get me out of this mess (this time)."

Pay attention to how your sentences are structured and look for ways to improve them. Eliminating the word "and" will force you to creatively replace that conjunction with a more appropriate word or words.

Use your thesaurus. If you're using MS Word, simply highlight the word you want to replace then press SHIFT+F7. Don't go overboard though because it will be obvious to your readers and will make you look like you're trying too hard. You can also use the thesaurus to find more appropriate words that will deliver the idea more poignantly.

When you're done editing, edit it again. And again. And again. Don't stop editing until you're satisfied with the final output. Check to see errors you may have missed on your last read-through. Again, don't go overboard or you'll run the risk of changing your e-book entirely and turn it into a completely different product.

If you're not too confident with your editing know-how and judgment, you have the alternative to hire a book doctor to edit your e-book for you. The fees differ depending on the caliber or popularity of the editor you choose. Some editing companies may charge anywhere between 2¢ to 5¢ per word, while others may charge on a per hour basis.

When choosing an editor, take note of the following:

Testimonials. Look for websites that offer editing services with REAL testimonials. You'll often see praises from fellow authors who include the titles of their books in their statements. Check whether the titles are actually being sold in e-bookstores and if you can, look at reviews or any mention about the overall structure of the book.

Prices. Don't just settle with the first editing company that you see in search engine results. Compare the prices of all editing firms that you see on the first page (at least) of search results.

Editor's Credibility. If you're faced with a choice between a cheap editing company versus a pricier one-man editing show, who would you choose? Now let's say that the cheap editing company employs freelancing journalism students while the solo editor used to edit for a publishing house, who would you choose now?

While pricing of the editing services is a major consideration, it should not be your sole determinant. Make sure that you'll be getting your money's worth and to do that, you'll need to ensure that your editor knows what he/she is doing. Don't hesitate to send an email inquiry about these issues.

Delivery Periods. Some editors may take up to a week to edit a 20,000-word e-book while others will only take 2-3 business days for the same book length. Always be clear with the editor on when you can expect to receive the edited copy of your ebook.

Other Services. Some companies also provide assessments, file conversions and ebook publishing aside from their basic editing services which you may want to look into. Look for companies that offer package rates that include a combination of two or more services to maximize your payment.

A quick Google search for e-book editing will yield results for companies such as Sibia, EBook Editing Pro and EBook Editor. Choose wisely and carefully to give you written work the best chance of being the next bestseller on Amazon.

Front and Back Covers

The saying "do not judge a book by its cover" may be a noble idea but in today's competitive book market, good visuals help sell books. E-books are no exceptions. A quick browse of the Kindle Store will show colorful book covers that are sure to catch a book shopper's attention. If you want your e-book to look legit and professional, take time in choosing the best artwork for your cover.

If you plan to create the front and back covers of your e-book, be guided by the following:

Size and Format. Aside from the e-book itself, your cover art will also be used as thumbnails in the Amazon Store and other e-bookstores. You need to make sure that even in a reduced size that the artwork will still be visible and your title completely readable.

The actual dimensions and format listed in the guidelines of Amazon are as follows:

For the Embedded E-book Cover or the actual first page of your e-book, it should be sized at 600 pixels by 800 pixels with a resolution of 300dpi (dots per inch). It should be saved in JPEG format and the file size should be no larger than 127 kb. Getting high-quality artwork in that small size would be a challenge but don't get discouraged.

For the Catalog Cover which is what browsers will see on the Kindle Store, the minimum width is 500 pixels while the maximum height is 1280 pixels. Use a 72dpi resolution and save in either a JPEG or TIFF format.
When you upload your e-book on Kindle Direct Publishing, you will also be asked to upload the JPEG version of your catalog cover. Amazon will automatically resize the image that you submit to fit their dimensions which may diminish the quality of the picture if you don't follow their guidelines.

Design Philosophy. As a general rule, simple is beautiful. No need to use ultra bright colors that may not appear as the same color across all computers and devices. Abstract artworks may serve you well while actual photographs may see a diminished quality when resized to fit Kindle devices. When including texts or blurbs, be selective with what you'll put in such a limited space. Also ensure that the title is distinguishable and readable even in small sizes.

E-Book Thrillers: E-book cover design for thrillers have it made. Simple and readable fonts, attention-grabbing colors and applicable for thumbnails.

Typography. The fonts you use for the e-book cover should be easily readable even in small versions. The typography can even be so unique that it can be distinctly identified with specific series of books or traced to a single author. You may purchase premium fonts online for unique typography or you can download free fonts and customize them further to fit your cover design.

Avoid commonly used (and scorned) fonts such as Comic Sans, Papyrus and Impact. Instead, try using Trade Gothic, Baskerville or FF Scala.

Easily Identifiable: Stieg Larsson's series can be easily identified through the common themes of his book covers which are made extra-distinct by the consistent typography.

Black and White. Most Kindle versions are in black and white so you'll need to ensure that your cover design will still look good in monochrome.

Diminished Quality: Mario Batali may know his way around the kitchen but we can't tell by the black and white version of his e-book cover. His name is barely readable and the top half of the image is hard to see.

Once you've designed or decided on the e-book cover that you will be using, let's move on to the final stages of preparing your e-book for publication.

Converting and Formatting

The final step to your publication preparation is to convert your file into a compatible Kindle format and to ensure that your e-book will appear on the devices as you intend it to. There are several methods that you can use to convert and format your e-book.

Method 1: Using MobiPocket Creator

This is the method that Amazon has posted in its guidelines for its e-book publishing. You will need to download the program MobiPocket Creator in order to complete the steps.

When you're done formatting your e-book on MS Word, save your file as a Web Page, Filtered.

Open MobiPocket Creator and under the Export From Existing File heading then click on 'HTML Document.'

Click on the 'Browse' button to search for your file. For easy reference, choose your Desktop as the destination in the Create a Publication in Folder field. When you're done choosing, click on 'Import.'

The left-hand side, you will see three links in the View box: Publication File, Cover Page and Table of Contents. Click on 'Cover Image' to add your cover art.

On the Cover Image page, click on 'Add a cover image' and search for your cover art. Once you've selected the file, click 'Open' and you'll be taken back to the Cover Image page. Click on 'Update' before you exit the page.

Once you have your cover art in place, click on 'Build' on the upper-right toolbar. Choose between the three encryption options. The most secure option would be Content Encryption with Password but it is also the least reader-friendly. In order to be able to preview your e-book using the Kindle Previewer, you will need to convert your file with NO content encryption.

Once the program is done converting your e-book, you will see the statement "Build Finished." If there are any issues with your cover art or table of contents, you will see a warning. If a warning is present, simply click on the 'Go back to publication files' link to restart the process.

You will be given the option to view your converted e-book using either the Mobipocker Reader emulator or the Mobipocket Reader for PC. In order to best preview what your e-book will look like in actual Kindle device, you can download the Kindle Previewer for free and toggle between different Kindle versions to see how your formatting will hold up.

If you are satisfied with the conversion and formatting of your e-book, you can now upload and publish your book on the Kindle Direct Publishing website.

Method 2: Using Calibre

Calibre is a popular e-book management book that can also convert your e-book into a Kindle-compatible format. One of Calibre's limitations is your inability to edit your formatting before converting without using a different program. Complex formatting may also get lost in the conversion process.

Before you can convert your file, you'll need to download the Calibre Software. After installing the program, you'll be greeted by the Calibre Welcome Wizard. You'll be asked to choose your language preferences and a file location where your e-books will be saved. On the next page you'll be asked to choose your e-book reader device.

Calibre does not convert directly from .doc or .docx format so you will need to save in HTML, RTF, PDF or TXT formats. For best results, save in HTML format. Remember to choose 'Web Page, Filtered' when saving your document.

Click on the 'Add Books' button on the upper left-hand side of the screen to add your e-book. Choose your e-book file on the file window and click 'Open.'

Click and highlight the file that you wish to convert. Click on the 'Convert Books' icon and the convert window will appear.

Before converting your file or entering any data, ensure that the output format to MOBI.

On the Convert Books landing page, you'll be able to personalize the metadata of your e-book such as the Title, Author, etc. This is also the part where you'll be able to upload your cover art. Simply click on the browse button to search for your cover image.

You can further adjust the different settings of your e-book output such as font rescaling options, heuristic processing and adding a table of contents by clicking on the tabs on the left-side of conversion window. You're free to explore these settings and you can restore your e-book to its original state by clicking on the 'Restore Defaults' button at the bottom of the window.

When all your preferences have been set, click on the 'OK' button to start the conversion process. Depending on the size or length of your book, this may take only a few seconds to a few minutes.

Once the conversion is complete, the new file will appear on the folder or destination that you chose earlier in the set up wizard. You may preview your converted e-book using the Kindle Previewer before publishing your product.

Method 3: Hiring Converters

The easiest yet costliest way to have your e-book formatted and converted is to pay someone else to do it. If you want your e-book to appear as professional as possible without worrying about device compatibility, this is your best option.

If you're willing and able to invest in professional conversion services, look into the following companies that are part of Amazon's list of conversion resources:

•	Aptara (www.aptaracorp.com) offers a wide variety of e-book services aside from file conversion.

•	Booknook (www.booknook.biz) specializes in fiction and non-fiction literature for all e-book platforms.

•	CreateSpace (https://www.createspace.com/Services/KindleReadyFileCon version.jsp) is
Part of the Amazon Group of Companies that offers file conversions for as low as $69.

•	Innodata Isogen (http://www.innodata-isogen.com/services/ebook) is considered as the leading provider of e-book service.

•	SilverChair (www.silverchair.com) specializes in medical content and literature

A quick Google search would yield a number of companies that specialize in converting files from different formats to the standard Kindle format.

It is important to get your conversion and formatting right to ensure that your readers will be receiving an e-book that's worth their time and money. When in doubt seek help from professionals.

6. PUBLISHING: THE MOMENT OF TRUTH

Converting and formatting your e-book is one of the most laborious (and stressful) tasks you'll be undertaking in the whole self-publication process. Once you've successfully converted your e-book into a Kindle-friendly format, the next big step you'll be making is to publish your material.

Compared to e-book conversion, publishing your content is a walk in the park. You have different options to choose from in terms of where to publish your e-book and where to sell it. This chapter will explore the most popular and effective publishing tool that will help you maximize your e-book profits: Kindle Direct Publishing.

Before publishing however, one important consideration you'll need to mull over is the selling price of your e-book. The price of your e-book will help determine whether your audience will be purchasing your material or not. If you price your e-book too low, you're risking losing potential profits and if you price your content too high, it may put off potential buyers from downloading your book.

Finding the perfect price for the length and content of your e-book can be tricky but we will be finding the right price for your work in the next section.

Pricing and Royalties

Pricing can be a challenging and confusing issue for writers, especially for first-time authors who may not know the ins and outs of product pricing. There are even ebooks available on the Kindle Store on how to price e-books for the Kindle Store - an indication of how important e-book pricing is to maximizing sales and how misunderstood this concept is.
Pricing Basics

To shed some light on the appropriate pricing of e-books, let's look at common pricing models that are often applied to self-published material.

Pricing to Penetrate the Market. Simply put, this pricing model aims to profit through selling in bulk or high-volume by setting the price low. You may base the price of your e-book on the price of competitors' materials to maximize profits and your audience. Many authors choose this model for a simple reason: customer loyalty.

This is a good way to get your first e-book a good chunk of attention from your audience and to establish yourself as a producer of high-quality content. Customers are 80% more likely to purchase from the same source if the first product they bought exceeded their expectations. This strategy will be especially useful for you if you intend to release other e-books in the future.

Premium Pricing to Maximize per Sale Profit. In this model, you will be setting your e-book price high (at least higher than competitors) which would guarantee a higher profit or royalty with every sale. The principal drawback of this model is that you will have a smaller market share as customers will be more hesitant to pay such a high amount.

If you are publishing unique content, with very little material available on the subject, you would do well with this pricing model. This can be effective to academic textbooks or scientific publications.

A word of caution though, premium pricing is not meant to be permanent. If for example, you are publishing an academic textbook about the history of ancient civilizations, you should think about lowering the price of that particular title after a certain duration or when you're about to publish a newer or more updated edition.

With a pricing model in mind, let's now look at specific factors that could affect the price of your publication. It is generally unwise to simply pick out an amount from thin air based on nothing but impulse, pricing should be thoughtfully determined to avoid over or under-pricing your product.

Consider the following features of your book:

•   Content. Is your content distinct and unique? Is it a fiction or non-fiction publication? Will your readers be able to learn a new skill or concept from your e-book? Are there exclusive images or artwork that was created specifically for your e-book?

•   Length. What is the word count of your e-book? How many pages will your readers receive when they purchase your e-book?

•   Competitors and Substitutes. If your e-book is too expensive, are there alternative materials that your audience can purchase? Are your competitors able to provide more affordable e-books? How many e-books cover the same range of topics?

A comparison between the top ten fiction and non-fiction titles (based on popularity) on the Kindle Store will show the following figures:

•   The average fiction e-book price is $4.13
•   The price range for fiction bestsellers is from $0.99 to $9.90
•   The average non-fiction e-book price is $5.06
•   The price range for non-fiction titles is from $1.99 to $9.99

As you can see, non-fiction titles are generally priced higher than fiction mostly because these are materials that will leave the reader with new knowledge, something that people in general are willing to pay extra for.

Another key consideration is the royalty that you will be receiving from every unit sold. Kindle Direct Publishing has two royalty options for writers: the 70% and 35% plans.

Kindle E-Book Royalties 101

In order to understand what each royalty option entails, take a look at this table:

	70% Royalty Option	35% Royalty Option
Minimum Selling Price	$2.99	$0.99
Maximum Selling Price	$9.99	$200
Delivery Cost	$0.01 minimum	n/a
Estimated Royalty	$2.09	$0.35

(per minimum selling price)

The delivery cost is based on the file size of the e-book in megabytes and is deducted from your royalty per unit sold.

As you can see on the table above, each royalty option has its own pros and cons. With the 70% royalty option, you will be able to receive the lump sum of your listing price but if you intend on adopting the Pricing to Penetrate model we explored earlier, your readers may hesitate on the $2.99 price which is your minimum selling point to get the 70% royalty. If you have a lengthy and information-packed e-book, $9.99 may be too low a selling point for you.

With the 35% royalty option, you will be getting a small fraction of your listing price but if you intend to profit from selling hundreds, even thousands of copies of your ebook at a low rate, you may effectively breakeven in a short amount of time.

Effective e-book pricing is basically trial-and-error. The good news is that Kindle Direct Publishing is flexible in allowing its publishers to change prices and royalty plans easily and according to their needs.

E-Book Pricing Tips and Tricks

As in any money-making endeavor, e-book publishing needs a fair amount of research and understanding in order to succeed.

Follow these simple tips and tricks in order to get the most out of your pricing schemes:

Check your competitors' pricing. It is easy to do a quick Kindle Store search of relevant topics and titles. Create lists or tables to compare prices and performance that you can use as a guide in pricing your e-book.

Read customers' reviews on Amazon. Popular books often have reviews on not only the e-book itself but also whether the price is worth the content.

Do a market study. This will give you an idea of what price your audience will be willing to pay for based on the introduction or preview of your book. You can ask your friends and family or you can do an online survey to broaden your research.

Follow the common rules in pricing. Notice how sale items always end in 99¢? That's because it makes people think that it is a bargain even if it's just 1¢ cheaper than the next big amount. Never end your price with 0 or 1.

Create bundles. If you are releasing a series of books or books that complement each other or are released in succession (think Harry Potter), create e-book bundles where customers can get a copy of all relevant books for a package price – has to be lower than the total amount of all books combined at a regular price.

You will learn more about the different ways to market and promote your e-book in the last chapter but for now, let's get your e-book published.

Kindle Direct Publishing

Publishing your e-book through Kindle Direct Publishing (KDP) is the easiest and fastest way to sell your material in the Amazon Store. Your e-book will also be sold in affiliate websites all over the world such as:

Amazon.com in the US
Amazon.co.uk in the United Kingdom
Amazon.de
Amazon.es in Spain
Amazon.fr in France
Amazon.it in Italy

Kindle app users will also be able to purchase and download your e-book to be used on their Android, Apple or Windows devices.

You will also be given the option to choose between the 35% royalty program and the 70% royalty program if your content is eligible (more on that later). On top of that, you can choose the currency you will be paid for your royalties, as well as the delivery of payment – whether via check or through electronic funds transfer (EFT).

In order to upload your e-book to Kindle Direct Publishing, you'll first need to log on to your Kindle account. If you don't have an account yet, creating one is fast and easy. Simply go to www.kdp.amazon.com to register.

Once you've signed in to Kindle Direct Publishing, you'll be taken to the KDP landing page.

From there, follow these simple steps:

Click on the 'Add new title' button on the top or bottom of the table.

You will then be taken to your book information page where you'll need to fill out all required fields.

On the same page, you'll be given options on your publishing rights and keyword targeting for better promotion. You will also upload the cover art of your e-book for the catalog and the e-book itself. When you're done, click on 'Save and Continue' at the bottom of the page.

The next page is all about rights and pricing. You will need to verify your publishing rights, whether it's International or in specific territories only. For original content, you may choose Worldwide Rights.

Now comes the money-making part, the royalty and pricing. You can now select between the two royalty options. With Amazon, the 70% royalty option incurs a delivery charge whereas the 35% option does not. The higher royalty option also has a higher minimum price but a lower maximum price.

At the end of the page is your compliance agreement. Tick on the box to agree with the statement and then click 'Save and Publish' to submit your e-book for KDP approval.

Clicking on the 'Save for later' icon will save all the information you've entered and selected about your e-book and its rights and royalties. When you go to your KDP landing page, you will see that your e-book status is in Draft status and you still need to publish your book for it to go on sale on the Kindle Store. You may still change the settings of your e-book while it's still a draft.

Remember that your e-book will still need KDP processing before it hits the shelves of the Kindle Store.

Once your e-book passes the KDP review, your e-book will then be made available in all Kindle Stores in different countries, from PCs to devices. The best way to make money off your e-book is to market and promote it successfully. The next chapter will explore the different marketing schemes and techniques that you can apply to maximize your profits.

7. PROMOTING YOUR E-BOOK

Congratulations! You are now a self-published author. Now what?

Just when you thought that your publishing job is over, you realize that there's a whole new world of challenges that stand before you: marketing and selling your ebook. Just because your e-book is on Amazon.com doesn't mean that it will automatically translate to sales. Writing a book is one thing, marketing it as something worth buying is another.

In this chapter, you will learn about ways and techniques on how to effectively market your book to your target audience and to increase your work's visibility both on the Internet and offline. The best way to sell a large number of your e-book is to let the public know that it's there and that buying a copy will enrich their lives.

Let's begin.

Online Advertising

There are literally millions of Internet users who log on to Amazon on a daily basis, making online advertising one of your best and most effective tools to spread the word about your amazing e-book.

Your Own Website or Blog

Having your own website or blog is a great way for your readers and customers to know more about you and your work. One of the many advantages of websites and blogs is its ability to appear on search engine results whenever someone does an Internet search for a related topic.

You can also use your blog or website to preview excerpts from your e-book or post glowing reviews and testimonials from individuals who have read your work. It is a useful space for you to get feedback on your work and to show your customers how your e-book can help enhance and enrich their lives.

Take a look at these helpful tips to get your website or blog to the top of search engine results:

Use relevant keywords. Keywords or key phrases are the words and phrases that are most frequently used to search for materials about relevant topics on search engines. Search engines like Google use these keywords to look for websites that contain the most information about that subject. Websites with the higher search ranking will appear on the first page of the search result, the prime location for any website listing.

In order to get a high search ranking, you'll need to use keywords related to the topic of your e-book in the content of your website. You can use the Google Keyword Tool (https://adwords.google.com) to determine which keywords are the most widely used for your subject.

Use the keywords in your e-book description or related articles that you wish to post on your blog or website so that whenever someone searches for a relevant topic, your website will appear on the search results.

Post articles. Posting articles related to the topic of your e-book is an effective way to generate traffic for your website. Again, you may choose to include excerpts from your e-book in the articles or teasers to amplify the interest of your website visitors. Include the link for your Amazon.com listing at the end of the articles to make it easy for your visitors to purchase your e-book.

Create an online community. Get your readers involved with the promotion of your ebook by creating an environment where they can share their thoughts and advice freely with other readers or interested customers.

Creating a blog or website is easy and there are numerous resources on the Internet you can use for free or pay a small premium.

For blogs, consider the following platforms:

•   WordPress (www.wordpress.com). You can access thousands of WordPress themes and layouts for free with an integrated stats system to help you target your marketing campaign more optimally.

•   Blogger (www.blogger.com). Owned by Google, Blogger has an easy-to-use dashboard with hundreds of add-ons that you can implement for free.

•   TypePad (www.typepad.com) A favorite among professional bloggers and small businesses, TypePad has thousands of templates and designs with add-on widgets you can use to enhance functionality.

You can also create your own website in minutes using free online web builders. Websites often have more features and functionalities than blogs.

Here are some examples of free online website builders:

•   Wix (www.wix.com) for Flash websites
•   Moonfruit (www.moonfruit.com) also integrates eCommerce options into their website builder
•   Doodlekit (www.doodlekit.com) offers free website hosting and blog integration
•   Weebly (www.weebly.com) uses a drag-and-drop platform that makes website creation a breeze

Alternatively, webhost providers also include website builders into their platforms even in the most basic price packages. For as low as $3 a month, you'll be able to have your own domain name and webhosting for your website.

Having your own domain name and e-mail address will give you a more professional image. On top of that, most webhost providers offer marketing credits for Google AdSense, Facebook Marketing and other online advertising companies.

Consider these webhost providers:

• InMotion Hosting (www.inmotionhosting.com). For as low as $5.95, you'll enjoy unlimited disk space, data backup and a website builder.

• WebHostingHub (www.webhostinghub.com). The promotional price of $3.95 per month will afford you unlimited website hosting and e-mail addresses, unlimited disk space and bandwith, a $75 credit for Google AdSense, a domain name and an easy-to-use website builder.

• FatCow (www.fatcow.com). For a limited time, FatCow is only charging $3.15 a month for unlimited disk space and bandwidth, a free domain name, shopping cart features, a website builder and up to $100 in advertising credits for Google AdWords and Facebook.

You may also choose to add video advertisements on your website or to include customer testimonials to entice your audience to purchase your e-book. The marketing possibilities with a blog or website are endless!

Social Networking Sites

In today's social networking age, it's hard to imagine life without Facebook or Twitter. Businesses and even celebrities have realized the importance of social networking sites and platforms in marketing their products (or themselves). Facebook alone has more than 800 million active users with up to 400 million logging on daily.

You can tap into Facebook's massive market effectively using two tried-and-tested methods: Facebook Ads and Fan Pages.

Let's explore both techniques briefly.

Facebook Ads. In a nutshell, you can post small advertisements with a 25-character title, a product copy with 135-characters and a 110px by 80px image on Facebook using their DIY ad generator or through the company's sales team (for budgets over $10,000).

Premium ads completed through the Facebook Sales team appear on a user's homepage which is considered as the prime advertising location in the site. Other advertisements will appear on any other pages except for the homepage.

Not Just for Skateboarding: Facebook ads can be created for a myriad of products and services, even your e-book.

You can also choose to apply Engagement Ads which are more dynamic than regular advertisements. With Engagement Ads, Facebook users can:

- Like the ad or the product
- Be linked to a Facebook Fan Page
- RSVP to an event
- Vote in a poll

You'll have the option to choose between two payment options: Pay per Impression or Pay per Click.

Facebook Fan Pages. Much like your own Facebook profile, a Fan Page will allow you to post photos, notes, status updates, events and videos. Your fans and followers will be able to interact with you and each other by posting on your wall or they can share your updates with their friends by sharing it on their personal wall.

You can post excerpts from your e-book, book reviews and even testimonials on your Fan Page to arouse interest from other Facebook users, or give Facebook-only discounts or coupons and contests.

To maximize your results from Facebook marketing, it is advisable to employ both methods. Remember to update your product description in your ads and your Fan Page information and status frequently.

Twitter is another social networking site that has proven to be effective in promoting a product. Twitter is a micro-blogging site that limits a user's post or tweet to 140characters. A tweet is broadcasted on the "Timeline" of a user's followers which they can repost (retweet) to their followers' timeline and so on.

A single tweet can spread like wildfire, making it the online version of the word-ofmouth advertising. Creating a Twitter account is simple and can be done in minutes. To tweet, simply type in your 140-character or less message on the "What's Happening?" box and click on 'Tweet.' You can also include images and links to your tweet.

You can tweet book excerpts, promotions, quotations or simply a link to your website or Amazon listing. You can also do Twitter-exclusive contests for your followers or hint on upcoming releases or future materials.

Gem in a Tweet: Neil Gaiman fans gushed about his casual Twitter conversation with legendary author, Salman Rushdie. And yes, he mentioned something about a book.

Social networking is a great way to promote and introduce your e-book to millions of people without spending thousands of dollars. It is an affordable and practical way to promote published material, especially for first-time writers and authors.

Book Reviews

Book reviews will not only give your e-book more credibility, it also encourages interested customers to purchase your product to see what the raves are all about. The Kindle Store allows shoppers to post reviews on publications that they have purchased and read. No matter how long or short the reviews are, it is undeniable that prospective readers are influenced by the reviews that they read.

Aside from the Kindle Store, you can also give copies of your e-book to blogs and websites that specialize in book reviews to increase your product's visibility. Blogs like Becky's Book Reviews (http://blbooks.blogspot.com) and Bookdwarf (www.bookdwarf.com) are visited by hundreds of readers on a daily basis. Getting a positive review from influential bloggers will help in the promotion of your e-book.

To kick-start the wave of positive reviews, you can ask your family and friends to write book reviews for you. Just be sure to tell them not to give any indication of any personal relationship with you and to use a different surname if need be.

Free Press Release Websites and E-Zines

Most bestselling authors have an army of staff who do the paper and legwork for them. A first-time, self-published writer may not have the luxury to hire a publicist to do promotional work for him or her. The wonderful thing about the Internet is that it is very supportive of the DIY movement.

With that said, why hire a publicist when you can make your own press release and have it published on press release websites for free? Small to medium businesses and startups have taken advantage of these free news release websites to great success. Established daily and weekly publications all over the world frequent these websites to search for news worthy pieces which is great promotion.

First things first though, you need a press release. You may choose to do it yourself (in keeping with the DIY theme) or outsource it to freelancers or writing companies.

It is advisable to keep two or three different versions per press release and to strategically post/release them in intervals, depending on your e-book's performance.

You can post your press releases for free in these websites:

- Free Press Release (www.free-press-release.com)
- PRLog (www.prlog.org)
- i-Newswire (www.i-newswire.com)
- 1888 Press Release (www.1888pressrelease.com)
- PR.com (www.pr.com)

Besides press release websites, you can also submit articles related to your e-book topic to Ezine websites in order to generate traffic to your own website or blog. These Ezine submission websites are frequent sources of content for newsletter editors, owners and writers.

If your work gets published in a newsletter or an online periodical, your public information will be cited and your website (or product) promoted. You can post your articles for free in select websites with more features available for premium and paid membership. The biggest Ezine websites are visited by more than 100,000 users per day, up to 60% of which are newsletter owners with their own email list members.

Submit your articles in these free Ezine submission websites:

- Ezine Articles (http://ezinearticles.com)
- The Ezine Directory (www.ezine-dir.com)
- Idea Marketers (www.ideamarketers.com)

Establishing yourself as a credible author or writer is a good way for your audience to trust and enjoy the content of your published work. There are more than enough tools online to get started on introducing yourself and your e-book to the world, take advantage of all of them.

Offline Advertising

Offline advertising should complement your online marketing campaign. It is one of the easiest ways to spread the message of your e-book across and to add a personal touch to the marketing of your products.

Offline advertising does not necessarily mean flyers, TV and radio commercials or door-to-door sales. It can be as simple as including the URL of your website or blog on your business card or through trade and industry road shows in your area.

There are two traditional offline advertising methods that you should heavily consider: newsprint ads and word-of-mouth.

Newspaper Ads. In the digital age, spreadsheets may seem like a dying industry but it is still an effective way to get your e-book title known. Ask your local newspaper about advertising rates or procedures on how to include your press release in the upcoming issues.

Word-of-Mouth. There is no better way to explain how your e-book can impact a reader's life by telling your customers yourself. Start small and think big. Begin with your family and friends and branch out to your neighborhood and your community. Give business cards to the new people you meet. Join local organizations or book clubs to expand your network.

Don't discount the power of off line advertising. While it is not nearly as far-reaching as online marketing, it can provide you with a group of followers that will be the first in line to purchase your latest release. Remember that the people you personally meet can recommend your product to their families and friends.

8. CONCLUSION

Writing an e-book is an exciting endeavor but as in any creative pursuit, it also offers a fair amount of challenges and hardships. Amazon and Kindle has made it easy for aspiring authors and writers to publish their own material through the Kindle Direct Publishing, opening a new world of opportunities for first-time self-publishers.

Many e-book writers face stiff competition in readership, as well as difficulties in marketing and selling their products. In the previous chapter, you learned about different ways you can market your e-book and to gain visibility for you and your works. The trick is to show passion and elevated knowledge in the topic that you chose to write about. The best way to sell your e-book is to show sincerity in your belief that purchasing your title can and will enhance your readers' life.

Don't back down from the challenge of publishing your own material. When in doubt, know that help is just a mouse click away. There are plenty of professional e-book editors, converters, writers and contributors on the Internet, as well as artists who can design relevant images for your e-book. Don't feel overwhelmed by the amount of work you'll need to do, it will all be worth it in the end when your e-book royalties start trickling in.

Remember to follow up successes with more materials to keep your audience satisfied. If your first publication does not perform as well as you expected, apply the lessons and experiences that you gained to your second e-book. Keep trying until you strike gold.

9. THANK YOU FOR READING!

Thank You so much for reading this book. If this title gave you a ton of value, It would be amazing for you to leave a REVIEW !

THANK YOU FOR DOWNLOADING! IF YOU ENJOYED THIS BOOK AND WOULD LIKE TO READ MORE TITLES FROM MY COLLECTION CLICK THIS LINK

CPSIA information can be obtained
at www.ICGtesting.com
Printed in the USA
LVOW12s2157240117
522066LV00001B/85/P